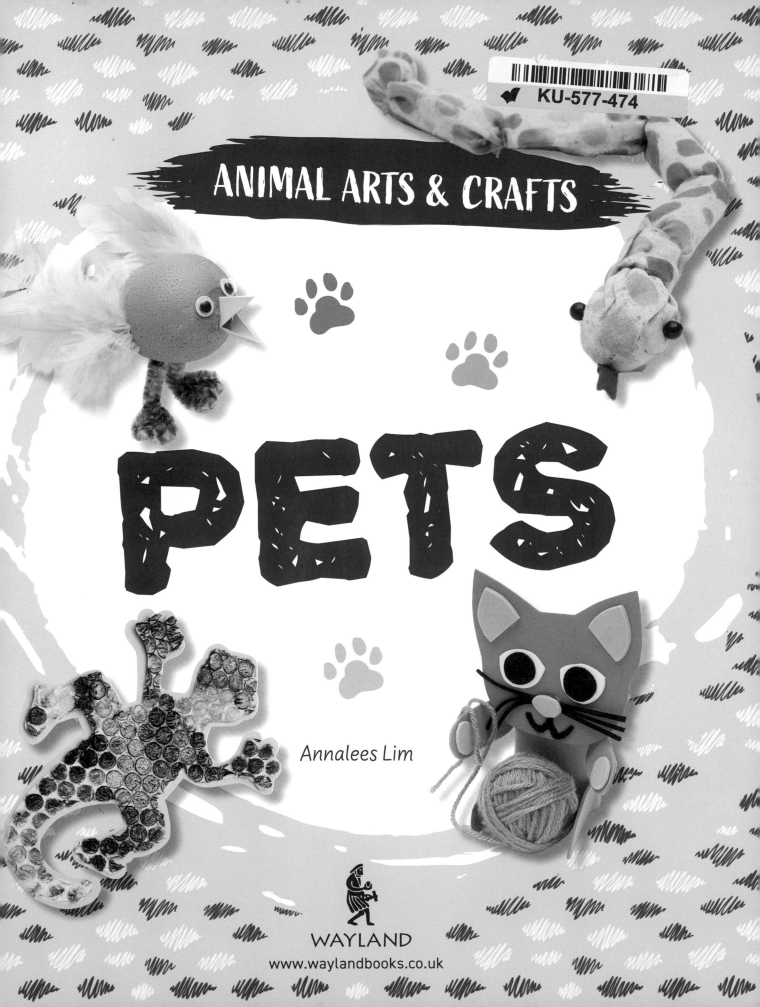

ANIMAL ARTS & CRAFTS

PETS

Annalees Lim

WAYLAND
www.waylandbooks.co.uk

CONTENTS

SAFETY PRECAUTIONS

We recommend adult supervision at all times while doing the activities in this book. Always be aware that craft materials may contain allergens, so check the packaging for allergens if there is a risk of an allergic reaction. Anyone with a known allergy must avoid these.

- Wear an apron and cover surfaces.

- Tie back long hair.

- Ask an adult for help with cutting.

- Check materials for allergens.

BEFORE YOU START

Do you have a pet?
Or is there a pet that you would like to care for one day? This book shows you how to make arts and crafts featuring pets, as well as telling you lots of fun facts about them!

Follow the clear step-by-step instructions to start creating your own pet collection. When you have finished making an animal, find out more about it.

A lot of the projects use paint and PVA glue. Always cover surfaces with layers of old newspaper. Whenever you can, leave the project to dry before moving on to the next step. This avoids things getting stuck to each other or paint smudging.

Some of the equipment or materials needed to make these arts and crafts can be dangerous if they are not handled correctly. Please follow the instructions carefully and ask an adult to help you. Now get set to make some animal arts and crafts!

HAMSTER IN A WHEEL

Hamsters usually sleep in the day and are active at night. This paper hamster can spin in its wheel all day long!

YOU WILL NEED:

- Empty cheese box
- A5 white paper
- Orange and brown crayons
- Wooden toothpick
- Glue stick
- Scissors
- Paper fastener
- Grey felt-tip pen
- A4 white card
- Red paper
- Googly eyes
- Black marker pen
- An adult to help you

Cover the sheet of white paper in a layer of orange crayon. Then cover that layer with brown crayon.

Scratch off some of the brown crayon using the toothpick. Make the scratches look like hamster fur.

Ask an adult to help you use the black pen to draw and then cut out a hamster shape. Add a nose, mouth and googly eyes.

Cut out a red paper triangle and stick it to the white card. Now cut out a circle of red paper, slightly bigger than the cheese box. Glue the paper circle onto the point of the triangle.

Use the grey felt-tip pen to draw spokes onto the cheese-box wheel. Ask an adult to help you fix it to the middle of the red circle with the paper fastener. Glue the hamster to the wheel.

DID YOU KNOW?

Pet hamsters need a lot of exercise! A large multi-layer cage as well as tunnels and tubes will keep it busy.

HAMSTER FACTS!

In the wild, there are 18 different sorts of hamster. This pet hamster is descended from wild hamsters that live in the deserts of Syria and northern Turkey.

A hamster can stuff an amazing amount of food into its cheek pouches.

GOLDFISH FACTS!

Pet goldfish can live for up to 25 years! There are many different sorts of goldfish. They all like to be kept in a clean aquarium with pond plants and gravel.

GOOGLY-EYED GOLDFISH

In the wild, goldfish live in groups called schools. Enjoy making these fun fish.

Mix equal amounts of water and PVA glue in a bowl. Blow up three balloons so they are no bigger than 7 cm long.

Tear the orange tissue paper into small strips and dip each one into the PVA-water mix. Stick them on the balloons until you have three layers of tissue paper. Leave to dry.

8

Cut off the end of each balloon. Glue some tissue paper fins and tails and a pair of googly eyes to each fish.

Cut wavy shapes out of the green tissue paper. Stick them around the inside of the plastic tub using a glue stick.

Press three chunks of modelling clay onto the bottom of the tub. Ask an adult to help you pierce the goldfish with toothpicks and stand them up in the modelling clay. Add small stones to the tub.

DID YOU KNOW?

A goldfish can be trained to do little tricks if you give it a food reward!

9

POM-POM CHINCHILLA

Wild chinchillas live high up in the mountains of Chile. They are very fluffy. Make your pom-pom chinchilla just as fluffy by using soft wool.

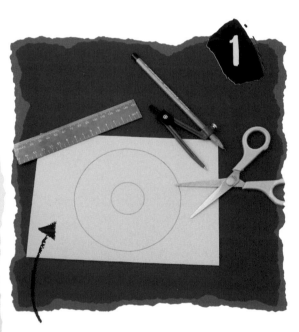

Ask an adult to help you use the compass to draw these circles and cut them out. Fold the A4 card in half. Use the compass, pencil and ruler to draw a circle 5 cm wide, and one that is 15 cm wide around it.

Cut around the pencil line, through both layers of card. Cut out the inner circles. Make a paper bobbin out of scrap card. Wrap grey wool around it, making sure it can fit through the small paper holes.

Place one card circle on top of the other and start wrapping the wool around them. Make three complete layers of wrapped wool.

Ask an adult to help you slide the scissors between the card circles to cut the wool. Wind a length of wool between both card circles, pull it tight and tie a knot. Remove the card.

Cut out ears, a nose, front and back paws and a tail from the felt. Stick them to the pom-pom with fabric glue. Glue on the googly eyes.

DID YOU KNOW?

Pet chinchillas like to live with at least one other chinchilla.

POSH POODLE

Poodles are not just pretty to look at. They are one of the most intelligent dog breeds, too. Make your very own smart poodle!

Mix equal amounts of paint and water in a bowl.

Soak eight cotton wool balls in the paint mixture. Take them out and leave them to dry.

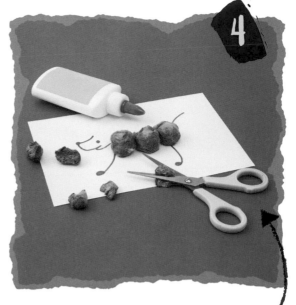

Take the marker pen and the A4 card. Draw a face, two legs and a poodle tail, leaving space for the body and the head.

Stick the cotton wool balls onto the card using fabric glue. They will form the ears, body, tail-end and cuffs. You can make some smaller balls by cutting them up.

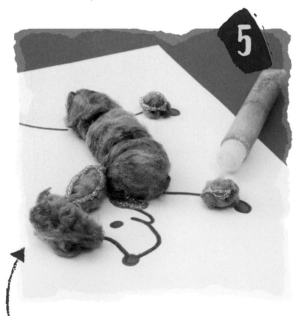

Decorate your poodle with glitter glue. Don't forget to add a collar, too.

DID YOU KNOW?

People originally bred poodles to collect up ducks during duck-hunting trips.

DOG FACTS!

All these dogs are related to each other, even though they look so different! That's because, thousands of years ago, people tamed wolves to act as hunting companions or guard dogs. All our pet dogs today are descended from those tame wolves.

How many of
these dog breeds
can you name?

PUG POTS

In ancient China, pugs used to sit on the laps of emperors. You can make pug pots to sit on your desk and hold your pens!

YOU WILL NEED:

- 3 toilet roll tubes
- Coloured card, 20 cm x 10 cm
- Brown, cream, and white paper
- Glue stick
- Scissors
- Black felt-tip pen
- An adult to help you

Ask an adult to help you with the cutting in this project. Cut two of the toilet rolls to be a bit shorter than the other.

Glue a length of cream paper around both of the shorter rolls. Glue brown paper to the full-sized roll. Now your three pen pots are ready to decorate.

16

Make lots of small cuts into one end of each pot. Splay the ends out and stick the pots onto the coloured card.

Cut out two cream 'U' shapes and one brown 'U' shape. Cut out four cream-coloured paws and two brown ones. Stick the legs and paws to a pot of the same colour.

Make a pug face for each of your pots by cutting and sticking shapes. Use your felt-tip pen to add details. Stick each face onto a pot of the same colour.

DID YOU KNOW?

Pugs have short noses. This can make it difficult for them to breathe.

BUBBLE WRAP LIZARD

A lizard's skin is dry, scaly and often brightly coloured. Use your favourite colours to decorate your lizard's skin.

YOU WILL NEED:

- Bubble wrap
- Glass paints
- Scissors
- A4 sheet of paper
- Pencil
- Paintbrush
- Thick, coloured card
- Glue stick
- An adult to help you

Using a pencil, draw a lizard shape onto the paper to make a template. Ask an adult to help you cut it out.

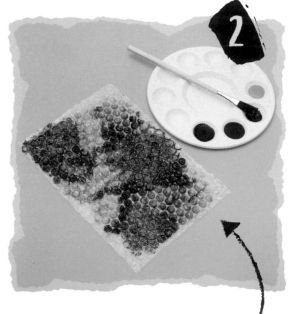

Paint a pattern onto the bubble wrap using lots of different glass paints. Leave it to dry completely before moving on to the next step.

Stick the template to the bubble wrap and ask an adult to help you carefully cut around the shape.

Cut a lizard shape that is a bit bigger than your template out of the thick, coloured card.

Stick the bubble wrap lizard onto the card lizard using a glue stick.

DID YOU KNOW?

If a lizard loses its tail when it is being hunted, it can grow a new one!

REPTILE FACTS!

People keep snakes, lizards and other reptiles as pets, but they need special homes, food and care to keep them healthy. Think carefully before buying a reptile as a pet.

Sadly, chameleons and other lizards are often collected from the wild for sale as pets.

You can learn about reptiles by watching them in zoos or in wildlife videos, or reading about them in books. You may be lucky enough to spot snakes and lizards in the wild when you are out for a walk.

Corn snakes live in the wild in the United States of America. They hunt rats and other small animals.

BEADY SNAKE

Some people keep snakes as pets. You might prefer to make this craft snake using fabric and beads.

YOU WILL NEED:

- 30 cm x 60 cm fabric
- Lots of small beads (no wider than 2 cm)
- Fabric glue
- Embroidery thread
- Red felt
- Scissors
- 2 small black beads
- Measuring tape
- An adult to help you

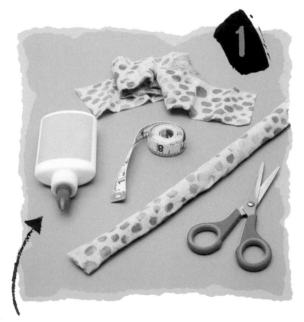

Ask an adult to help you make a tube from the fabric and glue the side seams together with the fabric glue. Also glue one end closed and leave it to dry completely before moving on to the next step.

Put two or three beads inside the fabric tube and tie a length of thread around the tube to hold them in place.

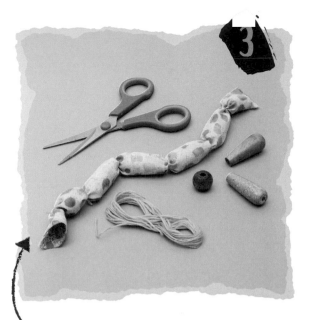

Repeat this for the rest of the fabric tube until you have 3 cm of tube left. Trim the end of the tube.

Wrap scrap fabric around a bead to form your snake's head. Tie the fabric together using thread. Glue the head to the body of your snake.

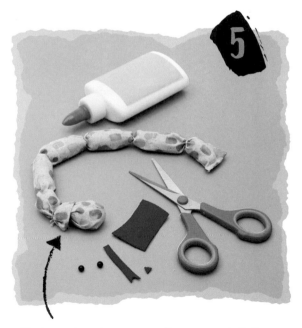

Cut out a tongue from red felt and glue it to the head. Glue the black beads onto each side of the head to form your snake's eyes.

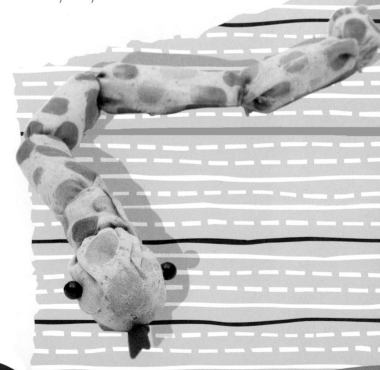

DID YOU KNOW?

Snakes can't chew. This means that they have to swallow their food whole!

FEATHERY BUDGIE

Budgie is short for budgerigar.
A budgie is a small parrot.
Have fun making your
model budgie!

YOU WILL NEED:

- Small polystyrene egg
- Coloured feathers
- Yellow card
- Craft glue
- Green pipe cleaner
- Light blue acrylic paint
- Paintbrush
- Scissors
- Googly eyes
- An adult to help you

Ask an adult to help you cut and bend the pipe cleaner to form legs and feet. Push them into the bottom of the polystyrene egg so that it stands up.

Paint the polysytrene egg blue and leave it to dry. This is the budgie's body.

24

Glue feathers to each side of the body to make wings.

Cut out two yellow triangles, one slightly bigger than the other. Fold each triangle in half and stick them on to form the beak.

Glue some googly eyes above your budgie's beak.

DID YOU KNOW?

Budgies are smart! They can learn how to say words and phrases.

FLUFFY BUNNY

Rabbits are born with their eyes closed and without fur. In just over a week, they grow fluffy fur. Enjoy making this cuddly bunny!

YOU WILL NEED:

- 2 large white dusters
- Ribbon
- Scissors
- Googly eyes
- Fabric glue
- Cotton wool ball
- Pink felt
- White string
- An adult to help you

Fold one of the white dusters in half. Fold the left edge towards the middle.

Tuck the right side of the duster under the folded fabric.

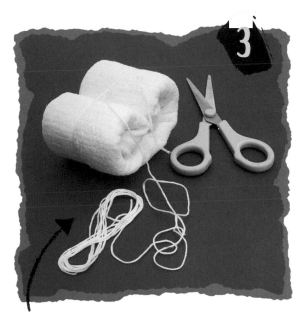

Roll the ends towards each other. Tightly wrap a length of string around the duster and knot it to form your bunny's body.

Tie off two corners of the other duster, using white string. They will form your bunny's ears. Roll the rest of the duster together in a tight ball. Tie the ears together using ribbon.

Use fabric glue to stick your bunny's head to its body. Glue on the cotton wool tail, googly eyes and a nose cut from pink felt.

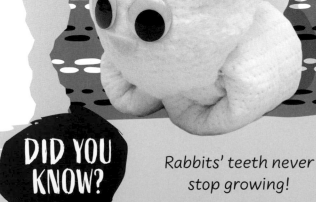

DID YOU KNOW?

Rabbits' teeth never stop growing!

BUNNY FACTS!

A pet rabbit needs to be kept with another rabbit or it will be lonely. Feed your rabbits plenty of hay, fresh greens and some dry rabbit food.

Pet rabbits need to spend time in an outdoor run every day. They love to run, jump and dig, so make sure the run is secure!

KITTEN FACTS!

Kittens are baby cats. A mother cat has between four and 12 kittens in each litter.

Kittens meow at their mother to let her know they are hungry or cold. Adult cats only meow at humans to ask for food or attention!

PLAYFUL KITTEN

Kittens learn to hunt by playing with their brothers and sisters. If you let a kitten play with a ball of wool, make sure it does not get tangled up!

YOU WILL NEED:

- Orange, white, pink and black foam
- PVA glue
- Scissors
- Small ball of wool
- Stapler
- Ruler
- An adult to help you

Ask an adult to help with the cutting and stapling in this project. Cut an 'H' shape out of orange foam, 7 cm wide and 15 cm long. These will become the legs.

Cut out a rectangle of orange foam, 20 cm x 7 cm, for the body. Cut a wavy shape that is 10 cm long for the tail.

Shape the rectangle into a tube and staple it together. Staple the 'H' shape to the tube and staple the tail on top.

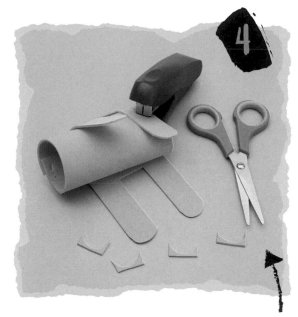

Bend the legs around the tube body and staple them in place. Round off the ends with scissors.

Make your kitten's face from pieces of foam and stick them together using PVA glue. Glue the face to the top of the tube. Add pink paw pads and place the ball of wool between its paws.

DID YOU KNOW?

Cats sleep a lot more than we do. They nap for about 18 hours a day!

GLOSSARY

aquarium a see-through tank for keeping fish, water creatures and plants

descended from be related to an animal (or person) who lived a long time ago

dog breed a group of dogs which are very similar, such as Labradors, pugs or border collies

gravel small stones

litter the baby animals that a mother animal has given birth to at the same time

reptile a cold-blooded animal with dry, scaly skin, such as a snake, lizard or tortoise

tame to train an animal so that it is not wild or fierce and can live alongside people

INDEX

First published in Great Britain in 2022 by Wayland
Copyright © Hodder and Stoughton, 2022
Wayland
An imprint of Hachette Children's Group
Part of Hodder and Stoughton
Carmelite House
50 Victoria Embankment
London EC4Y 0DZ

All rights reserved

Printed in Dubai

Some of the material in this book first appeared in *Creature Crafts: Pets* by Annalees Lim (Wayland).

Editor, and author of the fact pages:
Sarah Ridley
Design: Collaborate
Craft photography: Simon Pask, N1 Studios

Hb: 978 1 5263 2119 0
Pb: 978 1 5263 2121 3

MIX
Paper from responsible sources
FSC® C104740

Wayland is a division of Hachette Children's Books, an Hachette UK company.
www.hachette.co.uk
www.hachettechildrens.co.uk

Acknowledgements:
Shutterstock; Jan Bures 20; Cynoclub 15c; Goodbishop 28t; Eric Isselee 14br; 15tl, 15tr, 15br; Irin-k 6; Dorottya Mathe 15bc; Odua Images 14bl; Susan Schmitz 15bl; Slowmotiongli 7, 28b; Melani Wright 21; Dora Zett 29.

Every effort has been made to clear copyright. Should there be any inadvertent omission please apply to the publisher for rectification.